D1057104

the
doctordberry *show*

with co-host **Will Smith**

"It's your monthly dose for everything
Premed and post 'normal life'."

BE educated enlightened entertained

iTunes

USTREAM

doctorberry.com

doctorberry.com

doctorberry.com

doctorberry.com

doctorberry.com

doctorberry.com

doctorberry.com

doctorberry.com

doctorberry.com

doctorberry.com

25 tweets

Essential Advice

FOR PRE-MEDS

TIMELESS WISDOM 4THE AGE OF TECHNOLOGY

by doctordberry

iTalkinternationalinc

www.doctorberry.com

This book is designed to provide information and motivation to our readers and is intended as a reference guide. It is sold with the understanding that the publisher and the author are not engaged to render any type of psychological, legal, or any other kind of professional advice. The content of each chapter is the sole expression and opinion of its author, and not necessarily that of the publisher. No warranties or guarantees are expressed or implied by the publisher's choice to include any of the content in this volume. Neither the publisher nor the author shall be liable for any physical, psychological, emotional, financial, or commercial damages, including, but not limited to, special, incidental, consequential or other damages. You are responsible for your own choices, actions, and results.

Publisher's Cataloging-in-Publication Data

Berry, Paul S. (doctorberry)
    Essential advice for pre-meds / by Paul S. Berry, MD, JD, MBA (doctorberry)
        p. cm.

Library of Congress Control Number: 2011944940

ISBN 978-1-61348-002-1
1. Medical—Vocational Guidance—United States. 2. Medical College Applicants.
3. Premedical Education—United States. I . Berry, Paul S. (doctorberry). II. Title.

R838.4.B47 2012
610.71.173—dc22

Printed in the United States of America

Contents

While partying with my friends on New Year's Eve in 1979, I had an epiphany and something suddenly awakened within me. That night, I announced to my drug-addled 'friends' that I was going to become a doctor. There was uproarious laughter. "You don't even have a high-school diploma," one of them exclaimed. "And you're broke," another added. "Oh, I guess your parents will help," someone said, sarcastically. "I have it all figured out," I replied, defensively. "I will start college this fall, it will take five to six years to get a bachelor's degree, I'll then go to medical school and I'll graduate by June 1990." They weren't convinced. Nor did they really believe I was serious. I wasn't deterred though, and from that moment on, something inside continued to motivate me, inciting and provoking me, towards one goal – becoming a physician. I eventually graduated medical school May 1990.

I met with similar skepticism (though different reasoning) from other 'friends' and colleagues when I said I was going to write this book. Well, here's the book!

If I can do it, so can **You**.

1

GRADES and PMS

"To those of you who received honors, awards and distinctions, I say well done. And to the C students, I say you too may one day be President of the United States." George W. Bush

But, you will have a difficult time becoming a doctor. It's likely that George Bush would not have even been accepted to medical school. If you want to be President, go to acting school. If you want to be a physician, you must excel in subjects in undergraduate college that you may not have much interest in studying. Applying to medical school with a B+ (3.3) average is considered at the low end. I applied with a B+ average, though I ultimately graduated with a lower grade point average (GPA).

Remember, your biggest hurdle to jump in becoming a physician is getting *in* to medical school. To do that, you have to convince committee members that you have what it takes to complete the minimum requirements. As I will say over and over – once you are in medical school, you have a very high probability of graduating. You will become a physician. Your grade point average (GPA) is important. It is one of the top three considerations, along with MCAT scores and your personal statement, that will get you an interview. The reason I preach an ascetic lifestyle while involved

in the four+/-, year process of building an application through grades, MCAT scores and your personal statement, is because it is the most critical four years of your entire career. Stressed? Of course you are. All the more reason to follow the advice in these 25 tweets. Also, do not – I repeat – do not bother taking additional classes in sciences that will 'help' you in medical school. If you are a science genius and naturally obtain straight A's in these classes with little effort, then go ahead, take them in order to pump up and/or maintain your GPA. For most of you, science classes are interesting, you like them, and you, somewhat masochistically, enjoy studying them. BUT, also, they require more time, usually have associated laboratory time and write-ups and there are much easier A's to obtain elsewhere, such as on 'North Campus,' as we used to say at UCLA, or in classes with 'econ' majors. All with the added benefit of providing you with some necessary exposure to another world of arts, humanities, etc., which will, ultimately, make you a better, more empathetic and understanding physician.

As an aside – 'North Campus,' at least in the late 1980s (OMG, was it really that long ago? God help me!) was and likely still is where all the theater majors and 'artsy' types hang out. I had to take a class there in my last quarter, summer school, in order to graduate, and right before matriculating to medical school (boy, that still feels good to say, and you will say it too) at George Washington University in Washington D.C. that August, 1986. I'm ashamed to say, it was truly the first time I had seen UCLA's sculpture garden. It was the first time I'd left the area of 'South Campus,' (which was where the medical center was and where all the science and *REAL* college courses were taught) and, much to my surprise, I loved it! North Campus was a terrific experience, and the students were 'different'- not the pre-med gunner/nerds I had been absorbed with for years. You'll recall from my New Year's Eve epiphany that, prior to college, I was not only a high-school dropout but also a party boy. Now, before the arts majors flip out over an assumed accusation, let me say that there were also some very serious students on 'North Campus'. The difference was that they were studying subjects that were really fun! For instance, theatrical performance was, to me, fun, and theater history was interesting, certainly more interesting for me than U.S. history! I tell this story only to let you know that I was too narrow-minded, too much a 'pre-med', too much self-victimized by 'Pre-Med Syndrome' (PMS), and too self-important during those years. I realized all this by being forced to fulfill my breadth requirements at that pressure cooker university in order to obtain my Bachelor of Science in psychobiology.

So, doctor heal thyself, treat your own PMS by exploring your college's 'North Campus' and obtain a well-rounded education while concurrently racking up some more A's for your application's GPA submission. Yes, I know, you can take the doctor away from being a pre-med, but you can't take the pre-med away from the doctor.

2 MCAT – Scaredy Cat

"Boy, you said it, Chewie…Where did you dig up that old fossil? No reward is worth this." Han Solo, Star Wars, Episode IV, A New Hope, 1977

"What does this old fossil know about taking the Medical College Admissions Test (MCAT) today?" you might be asking. "Well, a few things," is the answer, because I was in your situation 25 years ago. The theory of relativity hasn't changed. Newton's second law, that force equals mass times acceleration

$$F = ma$$

hasn't changed. An acid plus a base still yields a salt plus water. Hello? !*

Okay, here's an important number.

$$260$$

That's the number of minutes you have to take the MCAT; 260 minutes, or 4 hours 20 minutes.

However you look at it, it's one of the most important and, for most of you, probably *the* most important four+ hours of your life. Why sugarcoat it? It's horrible. It's grueling. It isn't fair.

This single exam, this one day, as unfair and unjust as it is, will equal all the years you've studied to build your GPA. It will augment a poor GPA and take away from a stellar GPA, and vice versa. Many medical schools give the MCAT score equal weighting with your GPA, a few give it more, and a few give it less.

You must give this exam your best effort and prepare in advance. I would recommend 3–4 months to prepare. More than that and you will forget important material, and less than that will likely leave you taking shortcuts and with material not yet covered. Some of you will have a natural (or should I say unnatural) ability to do little study and score all 15's on this exam. You probably scored well on past standardized exams. Lucky you. Good for you. Godspeed to you. No reason to read any further here then, so move along and don't waste your time. Go to the exercise tweet instead. For the rest of you mere mortals, there are some tidbits here that may help. It's a test to help determine whether you can cut it in med school. It is the first of a lifetime of medically related standardized tests. Nothing prepared me for the rigors of medical school. Nothing.

As much as I hate admitting it, the MCAT does test an important component of an individual's aptitude, motivation, and ability to memorize and synthesize vast amounts of information – traits required to endure the medical school experience. How did I do? Well, we had the same 1–15 scoring, but it was six scores, if I remember correctly. I am attempting to obtain my old scores as of this writing. As I recall, it was three 9s and three 10s. Not very good, considering the competition. Now, forgive me, you may think I'm a sell-out, but…I took the Kaplan course.

Yes, I did. I also took it for the LSAT. Why? (I took it for the LSAT simply because I was too busy and didn't care about the cost.) Because I was so scared of the MCAT that I didn't trust myself to be able to put together all the correct study materials and study them in the most logical and time-efficient order. I didn't trust myself to be disciplined enough to study enough to get an acceptable score. I preferred to get a job and pay the extra money and at least have the peace of mind that 'somebody' had thoroughly researched, reviewed, and revised all the must-know information. I had confidence in 'them.' (At this point I am singing the song from *The Sound of Music,* I Have Confidence.) *How would they stay in business if they didn't know more than me?* I rationalized. This was before I had obtained my MBA, before Enron, and before 'QE2' – quantitative easing.

Besides, what's a few thousand dollars in the big scheme of life and your career? AND, as I recently told a student who was bellyaching about "spending all that money for Kaplan," if **You** worship money that much, then **You** should probably get an MBA and go into banking as a mergers and acquisitions specialist, not medicine.

I still recommend Kaplan, and I believe they do as promised, as long as you do what they tell you, and assuming you have the overall aptitude for the course material, aptitude that is already reflected in your grades for those courses at Kaplan prior to reaching the MCAT phase. So, bite the bullet, spend the money, and do what they tell you. Take Kaplan; it worked for me.

3   PERSONAL INTERVIEW — THIS IS IT

"I never heard a single word about you,"
is one of the lines in Michael Jackson's last song, *This Is It.*

Don't let this most important meeting, most likely the single most important 'interview' of your life, turn out like Michael Jackson's song. Don't let it be **Your** swan song. Don't let what happened to me, happen to **You**! Before I brief you on what to do, here's what I did wrong.

I totally blew my first interview. I droned on and on about issues that really didn't matter to me. I guess at some point I was just a talking head. Yet, when I left the University of Chicago building in the early afternoon on a cool, sunny autumn day and climbed into my economy rental car, I told my friend that it had gone well. I had rehearsed for days. I'd said all the right things. I'd even told them that I wanted to be a doctor to help people. I told them that I was initially motivated by working in a research lab at UCLA, where we were culturing a virus then called HTLV-III (later to become known as HIV-1), and that Dr. So and So was like a mentor to me.

When asked who I would like to pattern my life after, I said Dr. So and So because he was involved in the discovery of HTLV-III. Bullshit!!!

All of it was crap. I hated Dr. So and So. He was an asshole!

It took many days of replaying that interview over and over in my head before I realized how awful it really was. So awful, in fact, that I wasn't surprised that the thin envelope containing the rejection letter was waiting for me in the mailbox by the time I returned home the following week.

Just a quick aside here on the mailbox. I don't like thin 9" x 4" envelopes (nor do I like receiving certified, return-receipt-requested letters). Neither will **You**. Acceptance letters are not sent by themselves in small envelopes. I know this because I've actually received a few. Rejection letters are usually sent singularly. I know that because I've received dozens. I only wish I'd retained all of them so that I could reprint them here to demonstrate all the rejection I suffered during the fall of 1985. It was horrible. Oh, I've had lots more rejection and many failures since then too, and so will you, but the rejection from medical school, especially after an interview, is devastating.

Since I had applied to 40+ schools, lots of mail arrived each week. I would collect all the 'thin' envelopes (after the first few times of gleefully opening these 'thin' envelopes a Pavlovian response was created — open the mailbox, see the medical school return address on the letter, feel that thrill of being asked for an interview, because what else would the medical school be sending me a letter for, pull the thin envelope out of the mailbox, joyfully open it right there, then feel the heartbreak to read 'Thanks but no thanks' — after a few of these, you get it...a Pavlovian response to the thin envelope) at the end of every week and have a rejection party and rejection letter burning with my closest friend and a pitcher of margaritas. It was usually on Friday. I would stop at the store on the way home from UCLA, buy a fifth of Cuervo Gold (I spared no expense), fresh strawberries, fresh limes and a bag of crushed ice (the ice cubes from the freezer were just not acceptable), mix and drink. I had a Bic lighter (hmmm) and would sit there on the steps of the ratty apartment building in Van Nuys, California and read and burn each one, one at a time. Not a good coping mechanism. DO NOT TRY THIS AT HOME! (Or anywhere else, for that matter.) I wasn't strong enough back then to save them. I couldn't face leaving them undestroyed. There was something wonderfully cathartic about burning them, watching each of those awful, heartbreaking letters shrivel away, leaving behind an almost complete combustion reaction. I suggest that **You** save every one of them. **You** may write a book someday. As for the drinking, I never became an alcoholic. You may not be so lucky. There will be a lot of pressure during medical school and during your life as a practicing physician, so be cautious with alcohol. Now, back to the interview.

Mercifully, I didn't have any other interviews during that same timeframe, or I would have blown them all. I vowed to never again say anything during the interview that I didn't feel in my heart. I vowed never to say anything other than what I felt in my soul. After all, I rationalized, the canned answers didn't work so well, did they? Therein lies my first suggestion.

Due to financial constraints, most students attempt to schedule all their remote (like on the other coast) interviews on one airplane trip.

Do not do it! Unless you have already been accepted somewhere, or have had at least one interview to digest, or are a 4.0 from a snotty school and have 14's or better on all your MCAT subtests. If the latter is the case, you're probably not reading this book anyway. Do not read books on what to say unless that book tells you to be forthright and honest. Do read books on how to speak while remaining forthright and honest.

A little advance reflection would also be helpful. If you've spent more than a year writing your personal statement, your interview should reflect what is contained therein. Also, by the time you have your first interview, you should have a real, personal, emotional answer to the question 'Why do **You** want to be a doctor?'

The 2012 — 2013 AAMC MSAR mentions the concept of 'Distance Traveled' on page 40. I have talked with students who are ashamed, embarrassed, and distressed about what they perceive as 'skeletons' in their closets. For some reason, we believe that our life situations, if not like everyone else's (or at least like everyone else pretends), will disqualify us from medical school acceptance. Not true. Since many of you are under the age of 30, your perception and interpretations of your unique and sometimes painful past experiences can be limited by youth. Some of you do not yet see those experiences as the gifts that they truly are, especially when applied towards the field of medicine.

Think about your difficulties, your pain, your suffering…how have they made **You** stronger? How can they help you to help others? Keep in mind that, as a physician, you will be dealing with people at their absolute worst — when they or a loved one is sick and/or dying. And, at times, NOTHING will save them. Fame won't save them. Money won't save them. God, Jesus, Buddha, Shiva, Krishna, Allah, Mohammad, Confucius (pick a prophet, pick a deity) won't save them (or their physical bodies at least, arguably). When it's time to die, nothing, not even a doctor, will save them. But, **You** can still help those involved in death and dying. And, they will all turn to **You** and expect **You** to: DO SOMETHING, DOCTOR! All **You** will be able to do is draw upon your skills and potions to relieve their pain and suffering, and draw upon your experiences to help console those left behind. So, it's a good idea to begin synthesizing your experiences, especially the difficult ones, into useful sound bites.

Now, with all that said, here's the bottom line: Just like in the movie *A Few Good Men*, where Jack Nicholson hollers "You can't handle the truth!" many committee members will not be able to handle all your truths, especially if not properly packaged. Therefore, **You** must prepare in advance and do mock interviews so that **You** are comfortable handling some tough and provocative questions and so that **You** properly package your answers. Just like in media training where they teach you to turn every question into one of your three or four bullet points, **You** must take questions and turn them into answers that will focus on **Your** strengths, yet still be on point.

In Dr. Fleenor's book *The Medical School Interview* (which I highly recommend), he discusses the concept of 'Stepping-Stone Responses,' which is similar to what occurs in media training. **You** are able to gain control of the interview by subtly incorporating some memorized, canned responses/subjects into your answer while simultaneously being/sounding spontaneous. One must strike the delicate balance of being honest and forthright while refocusing the interviewer in the direction **You** want to travel with him/her. To repeat — the longer **You** spend preparing your personal statement, the better your interviews will be.

4   FEAR and CRUCIFIXION

"Fear is the Mind Killer I must not fear. Fear is the Mind Killer. Fear is the little death that brings total obliteration. I will face my fear. I will permit it to pass over me and through me. And when it has gone past I will turn the inner eye to see its path. Where the fear has gone there will be nothing. Only I will remain." Bene Gesserit litany against fear, from *Dune*, by Frank Herbert

Fear of Failure.

Studies have shown that we actually benefit from making mistakes (see http://www.scientificamerican.com/article.cfm?id=getting-it-wrong).

Young children are naturally curious, and approach new surroundings with wonder and amazement. New situations and new learning opportunities are readily confronted. Because **You** are reading this book, I can assume that you're at some point on the path to medical school. Maybe you're at the beginning of the medical school continuum - considering whether to be a physician. Many would-be physicians stopped at the point of consideration, and many of them would have been remarkable doctors. There is a wealth of wannabe doctors. Some of them are miserable, some of them have become wealthy, health-care 'Administrators/CEOs', and some have become other types of health-care administrative personnel/politicians whose sole purpose in life is to control physicians and the delivery of health care. We all know the type: the person who, deep down, despises themselves, but on the surface, as a way of channeling their self-hate, despises physicians. They don't speak it openly, but say it through their actions and via the medium of legislation. These doctor wannabes hate themselves because they didn't go for it. They didn't risk it. Why? FEAR.

"Do you want to predict your future? Then look to what you fear, for it will surely come upon you." doctorberry, November 10, 2010

"Our deepest fear is not that we are inadequate. Our deepest fear is that we are powerful beyond measure. It is our light, not our darkness, that most frightens us. We ask ourselves, who am I to be brilliant, gorgeous, talented, and fabulous? Actually, who are you not to be? You are a child of God. Your playing small doesn't serve the world. There's nothing enlightened about shrinking so that other people won't feel insecure around you. We are all meant to shine, as children do. We are born to make manifest the glory of God that is within us. It's not just in some of us, it's in everyone. And as we let our own light shine, we unconsciously give other people permission to do the same. As we are liberated from our own fear, our presence automatically liberates others."

The above speech by Nelson Mandela was originally written by Marianne Williamson, who is the author of other similar material. The speech by Mandela indicates a man who, during nearly 40 years in prison, thought deeply, read widely, and tried his best to understand human nature. In the course of that journey, he developed a firm belief in God, and by doing so, learned love for humankind followed by sensitivity, compassion, and an attempt at understanding all people, as well as the roles they played in his life.

Fear of Failure. Fear of Success.

So, they never even tried. It was safer that way. Back to **You**. If **You** have already made the decision to become a doctor, and you are now in the long, laborious progression towards that goal, some of you may be saying, at least openly, "Oh, I'm not sure if I want to go to medical school, I'm still taking my general ed to see what else might be interesting." The unspoken and haunting thought is really something like – *If I can get at least a B in organic chemistry, THEN I'll try to get into medical school.* And, although some of you will make it all the way to being accepted to medical school with that attitude, most of you will not.

I believe that our attention generates our conduct. **You** seek to accomplish something great. Greatness cannot be accomplished with a wishy-washy attitude. **You** must have a single-mindedness of purpose. Even if you are academically gifted and A's come easy, medical school and residency will expose your weaknesses. The training to become a physician challenges the best of the best. It is both a mental and physical marathon. It is also rewarding, exciting, and fascinating. Commit yourself wholeheartedly and failures become minor setbacks.

"Many of us crucify ourselves between two thieves—regret for the past and fear of the future." Fulton Oursler

So, don't become crucified between regret and fear. Go for it, and give it your all.

5

MASTURBATE!*? – ONHD! – Attenuate your SSB.

Mark Antony: "How can I ensnare you? What bait must I use to catch your love? I am your servant!"
Empress Nympho: "Ah, but the servant waits, while the master baits!"
History of the World — Part I, 1981

Some people actually gasp when they hear or read the word masturbate ... grow up! "OMG, MG, MG!! He didn't really say that? Is he actually going to make this a subject on getting into medical school? Oh no, he didn't!"

Well, yes, I did! Now just hang on.

Firstly, I must say here that I'm a firm believer in committing to monogamy when it is done for the right reason; when it is done because one loves and is in love. There's another *25 tweets* book in process about the differences between 1) loving someone, 2) being in love with someone, and 3) both loving and being in love with the same person. We often confuse the three different states of being, and this doesn't factor in yet another option, when we like but do not love someone, or love but do not like someone, and on and on that goes to the point where one has had numerous husbands/wives/lovers that have spawned numerous mortgages, children, and alimony payments. Blah, blah, blah, blee, blee, blee… So often, have I self-victimized. If only I had all the homes, cars, and furniture I've given away, I would already be retired! But enough about me. This book is about **You**. There's nothing more satisfying than a healthy one-on-one relationship with a person who is also your best friend. This generally proves very elusive for most people and, for some reason, rarely comes when we are looking for it, but rather usually occurs at the most inconvenient time in our lives. So, for those of you who are truly single, let's consider a few things.

 First, let's consider how much time **You** hemorrhage engaged in activities for one single purpose - Sex - Go ahead, add up the time per day/week/month/year you spend:

Facebooking your friends about getting laid.

Facebooking to get laid (oh, please, don't get prudish – would you feel less offended if I said "to meet people?" And what does THAT really mean? You meet people to get laid, let's face it).

Texting to get laid.

Dating to get laid.

Getting drunk to get the courage to ask someone out so you can get laid.

Attending social/sporting events to get laid.

Buying new/more makeup to get laid.

Applying gel to get laid.

Getting a haircut to get laid.

Rinse and repeating (ever read the instructions on the shampoo bottle?) to get laid.

Buying Axe products to get laid.

Whew, I'm already worn out. And the list goes on and on and on.

All this sex-seeking behavior (SSB) can take your grade point average and put it in the toilet. Not to mention the financial drain — money that could be used better elsewhere, right? Like pay for Kaplan. I speak here not only from vast personal experience but also from lots of reports from colleagues who, years later, admitted (they were in denial during the process) that they wasted many hours/dollars per week engaged in 'activities' that on the surface seemed benign, and in some cases altruistic, just to 'meet someone,' AKA: get laid. In fact, it's concurrently amusing and amazing the 'activities' some people will immerse themselves in just to get laid. I was speaking to a colleague the other day about this, and he admitted that he was on the crew team in college only because he "got more girls to go out" with him and, he continued, that "it was a numbers game — the more girls, the higher the probability that I would f--k one of them." Crude? Yes. Honest? Yes. Another colleague said the primary reason he did volunteer work at a hospital was because "if the nurses knew you were a pre-med student, they were a lot nicer and I got dates all the time because of it – it was better than going to bars and fraternity/sorority parties, plus they tended to be older, and I liked that…it had an added bonus of looking good on my med school application." He made me promise to not reveal his identity…ever. They both agreed that their grades suffered some because of their ulterior motives, but each justified it as necessary, and they rationalized by saying they were accomplishing other things as well – staying fit, building a good application.

But masturbate?!* you exclaim, appalled and embarrassed. Yes. Why not? It's already been demonstrated that abstinence from sex doesn't work. Yes, masturbation - It's safe. It's quick. It's reliable. It's cheap. It's efficient. It's drama and disease free. And, just imagine how much more useful, productive, study time you will have.

For those of you who are all hung up about masturbation, consider this. If **You** don't want to have sex with you, why would anyone else?

Finally, as a physician, you will be expected to be able to discuss sensitive subjects with your patients. What better experience than personal experience in order to understand and nonjudgmentally discuss issues with your patients. This also applies, though less so, to those in monogamous, committed relationships. Sometimes it's good to have a private, singular fantasy. Perhaps if more partnered people gave themselves permission to participate in occasional solo sex, there would be less infidelity.

Go to <www.doctorberry.com> and click the 'Contact us' link. Let us know what **You** have done, are doing, plan to do, to 'meet people.'

AND, the next time **You** get online with sexual intent, masturbate first. See how that goes for you.

6

BEER and OTHER INTOXICANTS

I listened to the following conversation in the emergency room a few nights ago, when some teenage students were having their blood drawn prior to being sent to jail. They'd been arrested for DUI (driving under the influence) and starting a fight with the cops. "We were like totally wasted, man," (like, he was now like, sober, right?). "Evan was riding shotgun but mostly he had his head hanging out the window puking all over his dad's Escalade, and Darrin was like careening around the corners with the tires squealing," the student slurred. "Alice was in the back seat with me, it was like radical, I mean, check it out, I was totally getting a blow job from Alice, then the fuckin cops showed up. Pigs. They asked for the registration and Evan like puked all over it and I think on the cop too. His dad's car is a mess!" the student reported proudly.

Does this sound at all familiar to you? Yes? Then why? Why are **You** engaging in self-destructive behavior? And I'm not talking about the blow job. "Oh, it's only a few beers, dude," a student recently replied dismissively. "Really? A few?" I asked. Do you have any idea how many times I've heard that as I look at the patient's yellow skin and abnormal liver function tests that tell a different story to 'only a few beers' over a decade or more? Where did you learn that it was okay to drink beer? What's the allure? Can't you watch a football/baseball/basketball game without 'a few beers?' It was learned long ago, I suspect. Imprinted perhaps? Your dad did it? Your big brother did it? It is an acceptable way of male 'bonding?' Girls are not excluded here either, but overall, they have lower percentages of such behavior (female acting out has its other avenues though). Let's run an experiment.

Let's count them one by one, truthfully. Let's keep a written diary (yes, I mean pen and paper, since anything electronic has a higher probability of becoming public) for 30 days. Write down every beer, 'obamashot,' jelloshot, shooter, Red Bull, five-hour energy substance, inhalation, injection, under-the-tongue substance, eye-drop solution (don't use Visine, please), swallowed tablet/pill/elixir (including OTCs). If the pages in your diary are anything but blank, then we need to talk. Are you already making excuses as you read this? Then we need to talk.

Don't get me wrong; I have always been a practitioner of 'Everything In Moderation (EIM).' BUT, I was lucky. I was a kid in the 70s when 'drugs were good and sex was safe.' It's only in retrospect that I realize how many risks I took, how truly lucky (if you can call it that) I was that I had a tendency to bore quickly, therefore never fell into a substance 'habit.' I did, however, use sex and food as coping mechanisms. That's the subject of another book, though. My point is — **You** have embarked on a path to a goal that few can attain, and that nobody — and I mean nobody, including Oprah, Barack Obama, and Bill Gates — can accomplish without going through the same grueling, labor-intensive, life-altering and profoundly rewarding process. Do you want to be part of a small, select group? Or do you want to be just another member of the fraternity/sorority? Habits like these do not improve with the years; they worsen. So, why muck it up and take away from the amazing experiences by blunting your sensorium? Still making excuses, still saying "It's only a few beers/bong hits," "It helps me relax," "It gives me motivation," "Blah, blah, blah, blee, blee, blee?"

Additionally, all the new neuronal connections that are required in order to learn and retain the mountain of information can only be hindered by throwing toxins at them in escapist, self-defeating behavior. The sooner you overcome, or at least moderate severely, such behavior, the better your life will be.

7

PERSONAL STATEMENT — WHO AM I?

Considering my mediocre grades and marginal MCAT scores, it was the personal statement that snagged my interviews. Had you travelled to 20+ countries by the age of 18? Do you speak, read and write numerous languages? Were you abused as a child, if not physically, then psychologically? Many of us in the 'helping/service' professions are from difficult backgrounds. That shouldn't be something that's hidden from you nor, if you're comfortable, from committee members either.

It's important to be able to demonstrate how your experiences would actually serve the medical profession, rather than having them thinking you're just messed up, and potentially someone who will take a place in their medical school but end up creating a vacancy by the time 1st year is over. Medical schools want people who can complete the required minimum standards. Once you're in medical school, it's highly unlikely that you won't graduate. Once **You** are in medical school, **You** will be a doctor.

The medical school faculty and administration do everything they can to ensure that no child is left behind - you won't become a 'matriculated but did not graduate' statistic. And your personal statement gives you carte blanche to tell them anything you want. So, what do **You** tell them?

 I discussed my turbulent background. I told a story and gave examples that revolved around the county home for boys, the foster homes, and the dysfunctional background that led me to the profession of medicine. Beyond that, I discussed how I was different from the other candidates with similarly disadvantaged backgrounds, and how I had grown and been made stronger by the experiences. I spent over a year writing that statement — editing, rewriting, crumpling it up, rewriting again, and asking friends what they thought.

The personal statement is one of those places where 'frenemies' come in handy. Brutal honesty has its place. Solicit the opinion of your frenemies. It will hurt, but you will eventually heal, and be better for it. Now, as they say in L.A., enough about me – (what do you think about me? Ha Ha just serious).

 The following are 12 personal statement mini-tweets on what to do, and what not to do, in my learned opinion.

1. Avoid political statements.

2. If you use religion, do so sparingly and avoid preaching. Take this statement seriously.

3. It should take a minimum of eight weeks to write, but a year or more is better (total hours > 40 minimum).

4. Spell perfectly.

5. Use perfect grammar. Hire an English professor or a graduate student to review.

6. Avoid relying on 'spell check.' It has ruined many great statements by including a correctly spelled but inappropriate word.

7. Use another person(s) as editor(s) and for reality checks (this is another reason a year is good, because you will likely have a few different people reviewing your words).

8. Don't try to impress anybody.

9. Be personal.

10. Make the essay interesting enough that your editor (and the committee member) doesn't want to put it down.

11. Do not lie or stretch the truth.

12. The essay should give the reader a Gestalt of **You**.

Therefore, spend lots of time writing this most important essay. The more time **You** invest in this statement, the better off **You** will be in your interviews, and the more you will know about yourself, which is always helpful.

8 NEVER, NEVER, NEVER, NEVER GIVE UP

"No! Try not. Do, or do not. There is no try." Yoda, Star Wars, Episode V

I often refer to myself as 'delicate but resilient.' Nothing has come easy for me. Nothing has been given to me. I have failed many times at many things, but I keep trying. I have found that tenacity, perseverance and courage ultimately reap great rewards. Many times I have thought about things said to me while growing up in boys homes and foster homes; "Who do you think you are," "No one gives a shit what you have to say," "Shut up," "You're a punk," "You're nuthin'," "You're fat, ugly and dumb," "You're just a stupid kid!" Yeah, great role models, huh?

I'll never forget what I said to myself at medical school commencement when I walked onto that stage and Dean Bowles handed me my medical degree…*"I'll never be stupid again."*

There will be many times when you want to give up. There will be many times when you'll say, "Frack it!" Well, that's okay. It's to be expected. We all have doubts. When you feel like it's never going to happen, like it's too much, like you're completely overwhelmed – take a break, have a piece of dark chocolate (addictions can form

here, so be careful), and better yet, exercise vigorously for at least 30 minutes. Those endogenous endorphins that are stimulated during and after exercise saved me many times (though not every time) from not only the fat farm, but also from booze, drugs, and unhealthy anonymous sex.

After all, if **You** never give up, how can you fail?

9   MSAR — THE BIBLE

As an aside, at the time of writing, I have not had any contact nor received any remuneration from the Association of American Medical Colleges (AAMC) or its representatives for providing the following information.

As soon as possible, you must — and I mean absolutely must — purchase your new bible, your own personal copy, not borrowed, not last year's edition, not the library copy, not shared with a friend, not downloaded, but your very own hard copy of the *Medical School Admission Requirements* (MSAR) from the Association of American Medical Colleges (AAMC). Publication Orders (www.aamc.org) phone 202.828.0416. At the time of writing, it cost $25.00 plus $8.00 shipping.

Don't step over dollars to save pennies. Don't make excuses that you don't have the money. Find the money. Get a job and earn the money. BUY THIS BOOK! Then study it, study it, study it! It is your new bible. And, if you talk with a fellow student who tells you that they read the MSAR and they didn't find it useful, they're either lying or they didn't study the book thoroughly enough. It contains a mountain of information, and its usefulness will not be revealed until you have truly digested it.

For instance: Upon turning the front cover of the 2012 — 2013 edition, you're greeted with a Timeline for Application/Admission that's…perforated (could you scream?!), so you can tear it out and put it in a sheet protector and then into a three-ring binder to carry everywhere, and also put a copy on your bedroom wall (after you've taken your iPhone, photographed both sides of it and made the appropriate page 'Use as Wallpaper,' then move and scale and 'Set'). And we're not even on page one of the Prefix yet.

As another aside: By the time I had acknowledged my acceptance into medical school (I still have the original letter, the most important letter of my life to date, framed, in fact just recently reframed with museum glass at Aaron Brothers, dated December 11, 1985 – what a glorious Christmas 1985 was!), my copy of the MSAR was torn, tattered, stained (with coffee, etc.) and worn from being taken out and then put back into my backpack thousands of times. I only wish I'd kept it for posterity, regardless. I still have my very first chemistry book of the very first college course I took that moved me from high-school dropout to, ultimately, Dr. Berry (and most recently doctorberry). I suggest you keep a few things like this as well. When you're in your 50s, you'll look back as I do now and have fond memories like mine, of for instance, an old, irascible chemistry professor, whom I shall refer to as Dr. G.

Dr. G was a wispy haired, face wrinkled from decades of scowling, walked stooped over, should have retired years ago, white male chemistry professor at UCLA who also taught general chemistry part-time at Los Angeles Valley College, where I initially went to college. One day, late in the fall, after going over our mid-term exam results, I asked to talk to him, in his office, after class. I had a 'C.'

"You know, Berry, you're never going to make it," he said. "You're too bothered with all the pretty girls (little did he know), all the 'extracurriculars,' and you're not serious enough." He went on, very Yoda-like and all-knowing.

"What?" I asked, hiding the incredible blow he'd just landed, which had all but knocked the proverbial wind out of me. I was already devastated by the 'C,' which I knew must have been a grading error (sound familiar?).

"Yes," he continued emphatically. "I have no hope for you. You'll never make it to medical school." I was speechless (a rarity, even then). "You need to lock yourself away in an 8 x 8 room, with no windows and no phone, and study, then, when you're hungry enough, study some more before eating, and keep doing that for the rest of this semester, otherwise you're through." With that, he picked up a pencil, dropped his head and, without looking at me, waved me away. I left his office feeling annihilated.

Take a look at tweet #17 and see the Fall 1981 grade for General Chemistry II. Yes, I got a D!!! That was Dr. G's class. The story is continued in tweet #17.

As for the MSAR and AAMC, entire books can be (and have been) written about them. For the purpose of this book, however, BUY THE MSAR!

10 DELAYED GRATIFICATION, weight loss, and a new word — 'REGRAT'

Achieving greatness requires, among many things, the ability to delay gratification. Obtaining knowledge, smoking cessation, weight loss, and physical fitness all also require the ability to delay gratification. We live in a society in which we want everything now. Nowhere will you experience this more than when **You** are practicing medicine. Patients will come to you and expect to be cured NOW. They want an erection NOW. They want to be pregnant NOW. They want to have a cold cured NOW. They want, want, want, NOW, NOW, NOW! Well, **You** are different. Right? Nay! "Oh yes I am!" you're now saying to yourself. Let's try a test.

You want to be a doctor, right? So, wouldn't you like to be accepted into medical school? Now? What a relief that would be. We're all wanting something, and it would be ignorant or just plain untruthful to say that, "Oh, I want to WAIT for such and such," (unless it's having a tooth pulled, in which case it's possible). But I digress.

You are reading this book, which means that you are most likely already engaged in some sort of delayed gratification. Likely you are in college – the antithesis of immediate reward! But, the gratification I speak of here, in becoming a doctor, is more than

just getting into medical school, and more than just graduating medical school. **You** are going to be delaying gratification for many years, and delaying many things, in order to become, and then be, a physician. "It's almost over," will become a mantra that will get you through many troubled and challenging periods. Perhaps you already say it periodically, like right before mid-terms or finals. The problem with delaying too much gratification for too long is that it can cause what I call 'Rebound Gratification (Regrat) Behavior.' 'Regrat' sounds like, and can easily become, regret. 'Regrat' encompasses concepts of becoming a physician for all the wrong reasons, wasting years of your life only to realize that it wasn't what **You** really wanted. Your mother/father wanted you to be a doctor, while **You** wanted to be a dancer, comedian, or any number of other vocations that did not meet the approval of your parents/peers/siblings/idols.

'Regrat' is the behavior that occurs when, even though being a physician (or anything else for that matter) is what **You** really wanted, you did not consider the required years of sacrifice, the required endurance, the required years of delayed gratification. It occurs in those not prepared for success, not prepared for the sudden life changes that accomplishing one's goals can thrust upon us. The typical person engaged in 'Regrat' behavior is now making money, sometimes lots of it, in comparison to their previously austere lifestyle of starving student, or starving actor/waiter/model. Their time has come. It is their turn to shine. They want it all, and they want it NOW! New car, new house, new husband/wife, fine restaurants, expensive wine (lots of that too, because if it's expensive, you are not an alcoholic you are an 'aficionado' — *please!)* and things and persons too numerous to mention. It would be rude to say Tiger Woods, so I won't.

Regrat does not occur in a child prodigy or child star — that's a different pathology from rebound gratification, since these subjects haven't yet had time to live, much less time to delay gratification.

We see 'Regrat' everywhere. Sometimes it's mislabeled 'mid-life crisis.' This subject will be more fully analyzed in a future book. For now, however, just be aware of it, and be sure that being a doctor is what **You** really want, and you want it for the right reasons.

Don't engage in the pursuit of medicine for all the wrong reasons, and end up regretting what might have been.

11

STUDY, STUDY, STUDY —
It doesn't get easier!

Here's a quote from the following online article:
http://www.gazettenet.com/2011/01/19/study-many-college-students-not-learning-think-critically

"Combining the hours spent studying and in class, students devoted less than a fifth of their time each week to academic pursuits. By contrast, students spent 51 percent of their time — or 85 hours a week — socializing or in extracurricular activities." (hmm...maybe trying to "meet" people?)

The study cited above is terrifying!!! Are **You** one of those? If so, it's unlikely **You** will be going to medical school unless **You** change your habits IMMEDIATELY (or **You** are an academic genius).

You not only need to study now to earn grades good enough to get **You** an interview for medical school, **You** also need to develop effective study skills to learn and digest the vast amount of information you'll be required to learn in medical school. I wish I'd taken a beginning Latin class prior to med school, because a significant amount of learning in the first two years of med school is based on Latin. My study partner in med school had been in a

seminary prior to med school, and he knew Latin from his religious studies. For instance, while I was busy trying to comprehend what erythema meant (and 1000's of other foreign words), he already knew, and was able to swiftly move through large volumes of information because he could rapidly connect word roots, prefixes, and suffixes to work out their meanings. Even today, I still find myself periodically looking up a word of Latin origin and wishing I'd used undergrad to form a small foundation in a primary language such as Latin. So, forget taking anatomy for now, because it won't help you in medical school as much as you think, unless you're allowed to dissect a real human body (and that's doubtful, since there aren't enough to go around for all med students, and so the colleges won't be giving them to lowly undergrads). Instead, take Latin.

The other subject that had to be self-taught was the ability to memorize vast amounts of information. I repeat — vast. Medical school (especially those first two years) doesn't require the kind of problem solving that college physics requires. Med school is more about remembering things, most of them in a foreign language with strange pronunciations (Latin). For instance: can you say, remember and recite the pathogenesis of: anosognosis, systemic lupus erythematosis or amyotrophic lateral sclerosis? It's much easier to say and know what these conditions are AND much easier to remember them if you know Latin and have solid memorization techniques. Mnemonics (if you don't know what mnemonics are, you're about to find out) will be your friend, will serve you for a lifetime, and will save you on exams.

Even today, I can immediately recall esoteric information such as DNA base pairing, purines and pyrimidines not studied for years (okay, decades) because of the power of mnemonic association that I developed while in med school. Therefore, I suggest **You** take some courses on memorization techniques. At the time of writing, I'm developing a *25 tweets* book about mnemonics. Check out www.doctorberry.com for updates.

Latin and mnemonics will benefit **You** more in medical school than will taking anatomy and other such courses in undergrad.

12

MD versus DO — Who Cares?

Well, back in the 1980s, I cared. I continued to be prejudiced for many years after receiving my MD, and only through decades of experience and decades of practice with many colleagues have I realized that it totally does not matter. I have known and worked with many MDs (Doctor of Medicine) who were marginally competent, and I have known and worked with DOs (Doctor of Osteopathic Medicine) who were brilliant, and everything in between, and vice versa. Today, there still remains some prejudice in our field, though much less than in decades past. There remains an opinion that the DO wasn't able to get into an allopathic (MD) school because he/she was not academically up to par. Embarrassingly, I too was guilty of this myopic and ignorant opinion.

Neiman Marcus *v.* Nordstrom
Tiffany *v.* Cartier
Apple *v.* Microsoft

One can draw any inference one chooses here. Personally, I prefer Nordstrom, Tiffany, and Apple, although anybody can make a reasonable and sound argument for the other choices, and have an equal number of people agree and disagree with them. That's

how it is with MD *v.* DO, in my humble opinion. The statistics can also be presented showing that one is easier to be accepted into than the other, but we all know what can be done with statistics now, don't we?

Instead, study the individual school's number of accepted students from your state and from your undergraduate college as a way to weed out those that are simply not interested in **You** on demographics alone. For instance, some schools have never accepted a student from California (New York, whatever, pick a state). Find out why. It's likely they're a state-supported school, and rarely accept any students from outside their state. Have they ever had a California (NY, whatever) student apply? Again, with the Internet, and website data so easily available to you today, this searching is much easier, and can be done any hour day or night, any day or holiday. I only had Monday to Friday, 9 — 5, and whatever the UCLA library hours were. If a DO school looks particularly attractive, then apply. Be prepared to answer the additional question of why **You** have applied to a DO school. It helps to understand the basic philosophical differences, which are beyond the scope of this tweet.

13

WHY DO YOU WANT TO BE A DOCTOR?

When it comes time for personal interviews, this will be the overriding question haunting you every single day. So, start answering it now. Write down a few answers without judging how they might sound to someone else, or to a 'committee.' Braindump, as I call it, everything that comes to mind. And I mean EVERYTHING. Let me help you — here are some answers to the question of why you want to be a doctor that most everyone has thought, at least once, but nobody dares speak.

1. I want to make a bunch of money.
2. I want to tell people what to do.
3. I want to be an expert.
4. I want to 'meet people' = get laid.
5. I want what Oprah, Barack Obama, and Bill Gates can't have.
6. I'm going to be a doctor, so frack all of you!
7. I want access to all kinds of drugs.
8. I hate doctors so I'm going to become one and then testify against them in court.

9. People will worship me.

10. I'm damaged, so I want to help others who are damaged.

11. I'm damaged, so I want to damage others.

12. I can play God, and who better than me?

13. I want to be a BAMF (uh huh, bad ass mofo).

I could go on, but, I'm betting that one or two of those answers may have secretly crossed your mind. So what? It's normal to have such thoughts. It's all about whether we act on them. Denying them is, in my opinion, the most dangerous option. Do you want to know my answer to that question? Yes, of course you do. My answer, though, will not help **You**. It floored most of the committee members. If you want to know, email me at <u>doctorberry@doctorberry.com</u> with the subject line 'WHY?' and I'll reply. Let me just say that the first interview I attended, in Chicago, I completely blew. Sank, drowned, got rejected. Why? Because I gave the answers that I thought I was supposed to give. I gave answers that everyone said were what committees wanted to hear.

In the movie *Miss Congeniality*, all of the Miss USA contestants are supposed to answer a question that has something to do with what they want most, and everyone gives the ONLY correct answer… 'World Peace.' Everyone except Sandra Bullock, that is. She says she wants stricter penalties for parole violators, and the audience gasps and goes hauntingly quiet. Bullock waits a second, and then blurts out, "And world peace." The audience sighs with relief.

You are not running for Miss America. **You** want to be a doctor.

There's a slight difference, and there's no correct answer. It's kinda like the Kobayashi Maru (from *Star Trek*). Here's what the committee members want to hear: THE REAL TRUTH!!! HELLO?? That's right. Why **You** want to be a doctor. There are myriad reasons why **You** want to be a physician, so here's my best advice.

1. Determine what your reasons are, then articulate them.

2. How can those reasons accomplish your personal goals while, concurrently, adding to the profession of medicine?

3. Give the answer in reverse order. In other words, ask not what the profession of medicine can do for you, but tell them what you can do for the profession, and then discuss how that helps **You** accomplish your personal objectives. Don't give that BS answer, "I want to help people." What's in it for **You**? How will helping people help you? The committee members aren't looking for you to be Mother Teresa.

"Being unwanted, unloved, uncared for, forgotten by everybody, I think that is a much greater hunger, a much greater poverty than the person who has nothing to eat." Mother Teresa

Take the time to reflect and ponder on who you are and what makes **You** tick long before facing any medical school admissions committee.

14 UNDERGRADUATE COLLEGE — Makes a Difference to You

Even though I was told that the undergraduate institution that I graduated from was completely irrelevant, I didn't believe '*them*.' In fact, I was so freaked out by my perception of the importance of undergraduate school that, after transferring from the community college to the University of California at Irvine, I immediately put in for a transfer to UCLA. In retrospect, I must say that I hated being a student at UCLA. It was grueling, and for the most part unpleasant academically, but I loved saying I went to school there. Also, it was a great place for everything except studying. Westwood was/is an amazing place for 'meeting people.'

When the Olympics were held in Los Angeles in 1984, it was a terrific atmosphere for a young party boy, but lethal for a pre-med. My transcripts show ample evidence of my trials and difficulties in the UCLA pressure cooker, as Dr. G once called it. Study the entering class profiles provided by most medical schools on their websites. What colleges did a medical school that you're interested in attending seem to favor, in terms of the greatest percentage of their entering class? I found these statistics to be very helpful, decreasing the number of schools I planned on applying to from the 60+ on my original list all the way down to

the 40+ to which I eventually sent applications. Some schools just didn't accept students from California, but some, you will find, seem to accept a high number of students from your state of residence and undergraduate college.

This is a time-consuming but important task. I kept the stats (we had no Internet then) of these schools on my nightstand for months, and studied them at all hours…a great prescription for insomnia. I also produced my own tables of what I considered to be vital statistics, most of the numbers coming from the MSAR and the individual school's entering class profiles, which was a much more difficult and time-consuming process in the 1980s, when there were no websites. So, there's no excuse for not collecting all the data **You** need to give **You** an advantage.

In selecting an undergraduate college, don't try to go to the big impressive name college for all the wrong reasons, like I did. Better to have a 4.0 from an obscure college than a 2.9 from UCLA. Better to go to a school that will encourage **You** to study, and have a broad academic experience, rather than tempt you nightly to go out to 'meet people' (uh huh, did you think I forgot? = get laid). And, don't forget, there's a wealth of opportunity to obtain good grades, pay very inexpensive tuition fees, have smaller class sizes, and more interesting professors at the two-year colleges. That's what I did, and it worked for me. Besides, I really enjoyed my first two years of community college, and it helped my GPA.

15

UNDERGRADUATE MAJOR
— Don't get PMS with this!

'They' really don't care what your major is. Get this into your head! THEY REALLY DON'T!

Let's look at some passages from the Bible (that's the AAMC MSAR, in case you haven't read that tweet yet).

The Bible says, on page 61, chart 10-K, that the highest percentage of accepted applicants, 50.0%, was for science-related majors. The first response is typically, "See, they do care!" But, let's not forget that statistics are a way to 'massage the numbers,' as they say in the finance world (I learned that in MBA school). There are more science major applicants than there are theater arts major applicants, but the numbers look more favorable for the arts when one looks at them as a percentage of applicants accepted. So, as with all statistics, one must be careful not to rely too much on any one set of numbers. Let's digress for a moment.

A few nights ago, I was called to the emergency room to admit a previously healthy, takes no meds, 68-year-old white female patient who presented complaining of left-lower-leg pain of three days duration, increasing in severity to the point that walking was

now difficult. She'd been brought in by her frantic daughter, who took me aside (before I had a chance to even eyeball the patient) and said, "Mom has refused to go see her doctor, and tonight she could hardly walk to the bathroom, so I told her she was going to the emergency room. I'm so worried. I just know something horrible is going on with her. Is she going to die, doctor?" (I really hate being blindsided by family members, especially agitated, frenzied ones.)

The patient's vital signs were: BP = 133/92, Pulse = 119, Respirations = 24, Temp = 99.0 °F (okay, pre-meds — what's the differential diagnosis?). There are a few worrisome things here. The most concerning for me is the tachycardia (rapid heart rate). The most concerning for the patient and her distraught family member is the leg pain. Since this is only a tweet, we won't go into the long, laborious discussion of deep venous thrombosis and the subsequent pulmonary emboli that can prove fatal.

Fast forward to me telling the patient (who gave permission for her daughter to be present, ugh) and her daughter, that the patient had a pulmonary embolus. I described everything in detail relating a lawn with sprinkler heads that get clogged (always try to use real world examples with your patients) to the blood vessels in her lungs and the treatment plan, blah, blah, blah, blee, blee, blee. The daughter's agitation escalated and she was freaking out. "OH MY GOD!" She exclaimed hysterically. "Is she going to die?" She asked me for the fifth time that night.

"Well, we're all going to die eventually," I replied, dryly. This, of course, did nothing to help the situation and the daughter's emotions were reaching fever pitch (expectedly… sometimes it's fun being obnoxious…I'm sorry, I can't help it….overly emotional family members make me crazy).

"Is she going to die tonight?" the daughter replied frantically. "What's the survival rate? Have you ever treated a patient with this before? Why aren't you doing anything?" She continued without taking in a breath." At that point, what I really wanted to do was slap the shit out of her (the daughter, I mean).

"You're asking me to predict the future," I continued, in between her rapid fire, panicky questions.

The patient, finally tiring of her daughter's interruptions (thank the baby Jesus), told her daughter, "Be still…let the doctor speak, for God's sake!"

"Thank you," I said. "Anyway, as I was saying, I don't predict the future well…or I wouldn't be divorced…twice, and I wouldn't have lost all that money in the stock market," I said. The patient was laughing, although the daughter was not very amused.

"You could take this a little more seriously," her daughter said, chastising me. "What are her chances, doctor?"

"I'm totally serious," I said. "The problem is that, aside from whatever issues you have with your mother, you want a number from me. You want a prediction. You are asking for statistics that would be meaningless, because if the probability of your mother dying tonight from this condition is one in 100, and she dies, it's 100% for her because she's the one. Now, who are we dealing with right now, the one, or the other 99 that will survive?"

I tell this story because, when dealing with statistics, **You** don't know which one **You** are, or are not. It's all a numbers game, so **You** must do all you can to help sway ALL the numbers in your favor, not just a single set of statistics. Got it? Good.

Major in the subject that **You** like the most, because you'll get better grades, enjoy yourself a little more, and have something interesting to discuss in your personal statement and interviews.

16 EXTRACURRICULAR ACTIVITIES—HELLO!?* This is NOT about 'Meeting People'

Depth, not breadth, is what's most important in this category. I had to work and borrow money to get through college (and medical school). If you're one of those students who is self-supporting, then say so on your applications and/or personal statement. Were **You** involved in activities just to 'meet people?' Were **You** involved in activities just to make your application look good? Or, did you get involved with an activity that **You** were truly passionate about? My application(s) had nothing listed in this category. So what? I had to work to support myself. That was enough. I thought that if I helped myself I'd be one less person needing someone else's help. So, be true to yourself. If you find yourself in a place where you can go out and do charitable work at the same time as you're doing your best to get into medical school, be my guest. Just don't put yourself in a situation where you think you have to do volunteer work and study at the same time, only to fail on both ends. Remember, you'll have plenty of time and money to be charitable after you have MD (or DO) after your name, e.g. Doctors Without Borders.

Polonius's advice to his son Laertes was, "*This above all: to thine own self be true, and it must follow, as the night the day, thou canst not be false to any man.*" Shakespeare's Hamlet (Act I, scene III, lines 78—80)

As for extracurricular activities, the most common endeavor here is some form of community service and/or volunteer medical/clinical experience. Personally, I would attempt to find a job, even one that pays next to nothing, because I've found that you're more valued by others when receiving pay for your services. Sad but true. Especially at your level. Sean Penn and Dr. So and So will get accolades for their volunteer work because they're Sean Penn and Dr. So and So. Sorry to all you volunteers, who do a wonderful service. God love you and bless you. If **You** are a trust fund baby, then please, volunteer. The rest of you…get a job.

Make sure you know why **You** are engaged in any specific 'extracurricular' activity. Know why you're doing it…or not. Know thyself. That's a lifelong journey; knowing thyself, so start now.

OMG! I Got an F!!! Or a D!! Or...Whatever ...Pick a Grade

There are other tweets that relate directly to this one. Be sure to read tweet #9 to get the first part of this initially painful (for me back in 1982), yet encouraging (for you now) story. So, there I was, in the fall of 1982, full head of hair, washboard stomach, 25 years young, in my first full year of academics at a community college in a suburb outside of Los Angeles. And, there was Dr. G, way past retirement, still tormenting young medical school hopefuls with his General Chemistry II course, a total of five semester units. My Los Angeles Valley College transcript (they are reprinted a couple of pages forward from here) demonstrates the *D* I received in General Chemistry II, and below that it states *Course Repeated Subsequently (Grade/Units Not Used)*. Since then, I've discovered that, in California at least, a student can retake a course and the previous grades/units are completely eradicated.

Catherine, a bright late-twenty-something pre-med told me her story. "I went before the committee to have academic forgiveness because, when I was still partying in my late teens, I just took an environmental studies class at the community college to see what it was like. I wasn't serious, and soon realized I wasn't interested in being in school, so I just stopped going, and never bothered to formally withdraw. That left an F on my transcript. Talk about slaughtering my GPA before even starting!" she continued. "So, now that I'm serious, and want to go to medical school, I had to sit before the committee and plead my case. It was granted, so I had a fresh start, a clean slate so to speak." This is what's called *Academic Forgiveness*, and it allows a student to petition and sometimes sit before a committee to state their case for a grade/ course to be removed from the transcript, like Catherine did. It wasn't so easy in my day (not to mention walking uphill to school, both ways, in the snow, blah, blah, blah, blee, blee, blee). Okay, back to me – the transcripts show that I had more academic issues than just General Chemistry — we'll come to those in a minute — but to continue with Dr. G: I went to see him one fine spring Los Angeles morning at his office at UCLA.

"Berry!" he exclaimed. *Well, I thought, at least he remembered my name, and this was L.A.*, where as long as they're talking about you or remember your name, you're doing great, regardless of what's being said. Death is, after all, no press at all.

"Yes, it's me," I replied.

After the usual pleasantries, which Dr. G was not very long on, he said, "What are you doing here?"

"I'm a student here," I replied, proudly.

"My God, what were they thinking," he said, shaking his head, not smiling. He was serious!

"I just wanted you to know that I haven't given up, and I *will* get into medical school," I said, self-assuredly.

"Humph," he muttered. "It's early spring, and you already have a tan, so seems to me that you still haven't given up your vices, and this place is a pressure cooker (I still use that line today — the UCLA pressure cooker). You know, Berry, I really wish you good luck, but even if you do get into medical school, I doubt you'll finish," he said, resolutely.

"You have too many vices, Berry. You're too good-looking, you get too much attention from the pretty girls (that again), and do too little study," he droned on.

Why am I here, why do I need this old geezer's approval, I thought? "Never knew your father, did you?" a little voice said in reply.

"I'll tell you what," he said, challengingly, "if they're stupid enough to accept you and you actually get through medical school…I'll dance at your graduation!"

Oh, wow, Dr. G, how kind. You better start preparing now you bast--d, cuz you're on, I thought. I refused to let him see me rattled, so I did an about face and walked out of his office — for the last time. This time, I was mad. And I mean furious. "That dried-up f------ SOB, that co--s-cker." The expletives continued for a long time.

The figures that are produced on the next few pages are my official transcripts, which I will use to illustrate the examples that follow.

Los Angeles Community College District

LOS ANGELES VALLEY COLLEGE
5800 FULTON AVE
VAN NUYS   CA 91401

This document is printed on safety paper colored with a blue screen and is official if it bears the seal of the college. Photocopies of this document are invalid. Any modifications invalidate this transcript.

STUDENT PERMANENT RECORD   PAGE   1

ID: ▓▓▓▓▓▓▓   NAME   BERRY PAUL S

		UNITS				GRADE	
COURSE NO	DESCRIPTION	ATT	COMP	GRADE	CODE	POINTS	TR

FALL 80 (09/15/80-01/31/81)
CHEM 010	INTRO GEN CHEMISTRY	5.0	5.0	A		20.0	SU
HISTORY 021	HIST OF RUSS PEOPLE	(3.0)	0.0	W		0.0	SU
SEMESTER	GPA=4.000	5.0	5.0			20.0	
CUMULATIVE (FROM FA'80) GPA=4.000		5.0	5.0			20.0	

SPRING 81 (02/02/81-06/20/81)
CHEM 001	GENERAL CHEMISTRY 1	5.0	5.0	B		15.0	SU
GERMAN 001	ELEM GERMAN 1	(5.0)	0.0	W		0.0	SU
HEALTH 010	HEALTH EDUCATION	2.0	2.0	C		4.0	SU
SEMESTER	GPA=2.714	7.0	7.0			19.0	
CUMULATIVE (FROM FA'80) GPA=3.250		12.0	12.0			39.0	

FALL 81 (09/14/81-01/30/82)
ENGLISH 001	COLLEGE RDG&COMP 1	(3.0)	0.0	W		0.0	SU
ENGLISH 028	INT READING & COMP	3.0	3.0	B		9.0	
MATH 004	COLLEGE ALGEBRA	(3.0)	0.0	W		0.0	SU
CHEM 002	GENERAL CHEMISTRY II	(5.0)	(5.0)	(D	) 14	(5.0)	SU
COURSE REPEATED SUBSEQUENTLY (GRADE/UNITS NOT USED)							
SEMESTER	GPA=3.000	3.0	3.0			9.0	
CUMULATIVE (FROM FA'80) GPA=3.200		15.0	15.0			48.0	

SPRING 82 (02/01/82-06/19/82)
ENGLISH 001	COLLEGE RDG&COMP 1	3.0	3.0	A		12.0	SU
MATH 020	INTERMEDIATE ALGEBRA	5.0	5.0	B		15.0	CS
PSYCH 001	GENERAL PSYCHOLOGY 1	3.0	3.0	A		12.0	SU
SPEECH 001	ORAL COMMUNICATION I	3.0	3.0	B		9.0	SU
SEMESTER	GPA=3.428	14.0	14.0			48.0	
CUMULATIVE (FROM FA'80) GPA=3.310		29.0	29.0			96.0	

FALL 82 (09/13/82-01/29/83)
MATH 004	COLLEGE ALGEBRA	(3.0)	0.0	W		0.0	SU
MUSIC 101	FUND OF MUSIC	3.0	3.0	B		9.0	SU
SPANISH 001	ELEM SPANISH 1	5.0	5.0	A		20.0	SU
CHEM 002	GENERAL CHEMISTRY II	5.0	5.0	B	17	15.0	SU

** PERMANENT RECORD AS OF 07/29/98 -- CONTINUED ON NEXT PAGE **

JUL 29 1998

ADDRESS TO:

BERRY PAUL S

▓▓▓▓▓▓▓▓▓▓▓▓

Vice President, Administrative

Los Angeles Community College District

LOS ANGELES VALLEY COLLEGE
5800 FULTON AVE
VAN NUYS   CA 91401

This document is printed on safety paper colored with a blue screen and is official if it bears the seal of the college. Photocopies of this document are invalid. Any modifications invalidate this transcript.

STUDENT PERMANENT RECORD   PAGE   2

ID: ▓▓▓▓▓▓▓▓   NAME: BERRY PAUL S

COURSE NO	DESCRIPTION	UNITS ATT	COMP	GRADE	CODE	GRADE POINTS	TR
	FALL 82 (09/13/82-01/29/83) CON'T						
SEMESTER	GPA=3.384	13.0	13.0			44.0	
CUMULATIVE (FROM FA'80) GPA=3.333		42.0	42.0			140.0	
	SPRING 83 (01/31/83-06/18/83)						
BIOLOGY 006	GENERAL BIOLOGY 1	5.0	5.0	A		20.0	SU
ENGLISH 002	COLLEGE RDG&COMP 2	3.0	3.0	A		12.0	SU
MATH 004	COLLEGE ALGEBRA	3.0	3.0	B		9.0	SU
STAT 001	ELEM STAT 1/SOC SCI	3.0	3.0	A		12.0	SU
THEATER 100	INTRO TO THE THEATER	3.0	3.0	A		12.0	SU
SEMESTER	GPA=3.823	17.0	17.0			65.0	
CUMULATIVE (FROM FA'80) GPA=3.474		59.0	59.0			205.0	
DEAN'S LIST							
	SUMMER 83 (06/20/83-09/11/83)						
PHILOS 001	INTRO TO PHILOS	3.0	3.0	C		6.0	SU
PSYCH 002	GENERAL PSYCHOLOGY 2	3.0	3.0	A		12.0	SU
SEMESTER	GPA=3.000	6.0	6.0			18.0	
CUMULATIVE (FROM FA'80) GPA=3.430		65.0	65.0			223.0	

                    *** END OF PERMANENT RECORD AS OF 07/29/98 ***

JUL 29 1998

[signature]
Vice President, Administration

UNIVERSITY OF CALIFORNIA, LOS ANGELES • UNIVERSITY OF CALIFORNIA, LOS ANGELES

UNIVERSITY OF CALIFORNIA, LOS ANGELES
UNDERGRADUATE ACADEMIC RECORD
Page 1 (CONTINUED ON NEXT PAGE)
02/14/02 (Transcript Date)

BERRY, PAUL (Name)
(Soc.Sec.No.)   RESIDENT (Res.Status)   01/04/84 (Admit Date)
u (Career)(Student Number)

OFFICIAL TRANSCRIPT • SEAL REQUIRED

COLLEGE OF LETTERS AND SCIENCE
PSYCHOBIOLOGY (College) (Major)

OFFICIAL TRANSCRIPT • SEAL REQUIRED

UNIVERSITY REQUIREMENTS
AMERICAN HIST & INST ..... SATISFIED
SUBJ A ..... SATISFIED

TRANSFER CREDIT
LOS ANGELES VALLEY C 7 TRM TO 07/83 65.5 UNT

UNIV OF CALIF TRANSFER CREDIT
U C IRVINE 1 TRM TO 12/83 11.0 UNT
T ATT T PSD G ATT G PSD GPA
11.0   11.0   8.0   8.0   29.2

COLLEGE: LS MAJOR: PRE PSYCHOLOGY
---- WINTER 1984 ----
ORGNC STRUC&REACTNS   CHEM 21   4.0 B   12.0
CALC LIFE SCI SDT   MATH 3A   4.0 A   14.8
FUND OF LEARNING   PSYCH 110 4.0 C+   9.2

---- SPRING 1984 ----
BIOORGNC STRUC&REAC   CHEM 23   4.0 B   12.0
CALC LIFE SCI STDT   MATH 3B   4.0 B+ 13.2
THE SUPREME COURT   POL SCI 171 4.0 B 12.0

---- FALL 1984 ----
ELEMENTARY BIOCHEM   CHEM 25   4.0 C   8.0
PHYSIC-LIFE SCI MAJ   PHYSICS 6A 4.0 B   12.0
ABNORMAL PSYCHOLOGY   PSYCH 127 4.0 A   16.0

---- WINTER 1985 ----
BIOLOGY OF ORGANISMS BIOL 5   4.0 B   12.0
HEAT-SND&ELEC&MAGNT   PHYSICS 3B 4.0 B   12.0 N1
  04/08/85 GRADE CHANGED
PHYSIOLOGICAL PSYCH   PSYCH 115 4.0 B   12.0 RD

---- SPRING 1985 ----
CALC LIFE SCI STDT   MATH 3C   4.0 D
  REPEATED, EXCLUDED FROM GPA
LIGHT-REL?&MOD PHY   PHYSICS 3C 4.0 C   8.0
RESEARCH METH-PSYCH   PSYCH 42   4.0 C+   9.2

DEGREES
BACHELOR OF SCIENCE
SEPTEMBER 19, 1986
IN PSYCHOBIOLOGY

---- FALL 1985 ----
DEVELOPMENTAL BIOL   BIOL 138   4.0 C   8.0 G1
CALC LIFE SCI STDT   MATH 3C   4.0 A   14.8
BHAVIORL PHARMACOL REPEAT OF CRABREKEN
                      PSYCH 118B 4.0 B   10.8

---- WINTER 1986 ----
(COLLEGE: LS MAJOR: PSYCHOBIOLOGY)
INTRODUCTRY GENE   BIOL 8   4.0 P   PN
FUNCTIONAL HISTOLOGY BIOL 153   4.0 C   6.8
HLTH CARE&CONST LAW   CED 125   4.0 B   12.0
ANATOMY FOR DANCER   DANCE 123A 4.0 B   12.0
COMPARTV PSYCHOBIOL   PSYCH 118A 4.0 C   8.0

---- SPRING 1986 ----
HUMAN GENETICS   BIOL CM156 4.0 O   4.0
GENET&REPROCT TECH   CED 121   4.0 B   10.8
PHYSIOLOGCL PSYC-LAB PSYCH 116 4.0 B   12.0
HUMAN INFO PROCESNG   PSYCH 120 4.0 B   10.8
HLTH PROM&COMMUNTY   PSYCH 127 4.0 B   10.2
HEALTH CARE-POLITY   PUB HLT M190 4.0 A 16.0

---- SUMMER 1 1986 ----
BASIC PHYSIOL&APLIC   PSYCH 195C 4.0 B   12.0
HIST EUROPEAN THEA   THAER 102B 4.0 B   12.0

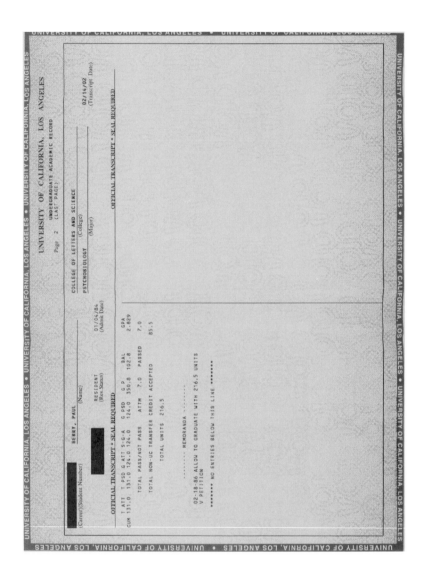

Out of 9 quarters at UCLA, there were only two quarters when I didn't have at least one grade of C+/ — or, OMG! a D! A total of 31 classes, each consisting of four units, of which only four had a grade of A or A — . *Maybe Dr. G was right* I thought, many times. I also thought that each time I obtained a grade of B or worse, it took me another rung down the ladder towards failure, another step closer to Dr. G's prediction coming true.

But, every B+ and better was another rung up the ladder towards acceptance into medical school. So, back to the UCLA transcripts. Out of a total of 31 classes, there were:

2 As

2 A-s

1 B+

12 Bs

3 B-s

3 C+s

4 Cs

1 C-

2 Ds

and one Pass

Geez, why did they let ME into medical school?

"Oh," you're saying, "he must have had great MCAT scores." No, I did not. See tweet #2. The bottom line here? If I can do it, SO CAN **You**!

In the early spring of 1990, I sent a formal invitation with RSVP to Dr. G urging him to attend and dance at my medical school graduation.

Of course, I received no acknowledgement, no congratulations… nothing.

Many students have a Dr. G in their life. Often it is a parent. Usually it is the father. I never knew my father, so, I guess I have a tendency to attract stern, emotionally distant father figures. They are akin to 'frenemies'. They are a double-edged sword that cuts deep both ways.

As for your grades…don't despair if **You** lack a 4.0!!

18

I'M TOO OLD —
IT'S TOO LATE FOR ME

"My own counsel will I keep on who is to become trained…he's too old, yes, too old to begin the training." Yoda, Star Wars, Episode V

"Bulls--t!" That's what I would have said to that old geezer Yoda, telling me I was too old. In fact, I was 29 years old when I started medical school, but it doesn't matter if you're 49 years old. I'm now 54. If I weren't already a physician, and really, really, really wanted to pursue becoming a doctor, my age would not stop me. Nor should it hinder you.

Let's all turn to page 63 in the Bible (that's the AAMC MSAR, in case you haven't read that tweet yet), second paragraph, second verse, and read together in unison: "Accepted applicants for the 2010 entering class were between 17 and 57 years of age at the time of expected matriculation."

Age is irrelevant. Resistance is futile. Do **You** want to become a doctor? THEN DO IT!

19 VISUALIZATION — The Key to Controlling Your Thoughts and Realizing Your Destiny

Creative visualization is a simple yet effective way of communicating with the subconscious mind. If you have watched, read, or heard about *The Secret* (which, by the way, was nothing original), the power of the subconscious mind (or God, Jesus, Buddha, Allah, Shiva, whatever makes you happy) is capable of empowering an individual to attract and attain the things he/she desires. Creative visualization is simply the process of forming mental images in our mind's eye and making them come true. And, once learned and properly practiced, this process can easily be completed in just 5 — 10 minutes each day, and yet I believe it can create powerful results in one's life. It has in mine, and it can in yours.

Everything you see around you started with a thought. The book or computer you have in your hands, the chair you're sitting on, the minuscule fiber that makes up the clothing you're wearing. Visualization is a great way to keep your thoughts in focus. Creative visualization is a better, more efficient way to control where to focus your thoughts. If you turn on the TV, your focus will be all over the place, e.g., 30 seconds on a car commercial, 30 seconds on prescription medication, 60 seconds on car insurance, 10 minutes on the program you're watching, then more commercials, and so on. You've completely relinquished control of your life to someone else. 'They' are telling you what to think about. By default, you're not in the driver's seat anymore.

If you want to accomplish something great, you have to focus on the thing you want to accomplish. Creative visualization puts you back in control. And you can do it in only ten minutes a day. Let's use the goal of being a physician. You may want to start with getting accepted into medical school, or some other step in the process.

First, find a tranquil place where you won't be disturbed.

Second, close your eyes and take a few deep breaths.

Third, visualize yourself as a successful practicing physician. Include as many details as possible. Are you in your own private office, or in a hospital? How is it decorated? Is there any music playing? What does it smell like? What kind of shoes and clothing are you wearing (include color, brand, etc.). See and hear people referring to **You** as doctor. Is there a stethoscope around your neck?

Remember: Visualize what **You** want, not what you think you deserve, not what you think is possible. Focus on what **You** want, even if it seems impossible.

Be creative; don't limit yourself to what you know now. Everything is possible. You can apply this to anything you want in life. Just go for it! But remember: there are 1,440 minutes in a day, and it's up to you, and you alone, what **You** do with those 1,440 minutes. Do this exercise for five minutes twice a day, every day. There will still be 1,430 minutes each day for other activities.

Spend time learning and doing visualization. This exercise will give you more bang for your buck than any other activity. Learn it. Practice it. Make it a habit....serve **You** well, it will.

20

EXERCISE — Ewwww!

When I was an undergraduate, I would combine jogging with visualization to create a meditation-like state and, being type-A, kill two birds with one stone. Each mile I jogged, I would see myself performing perfectly at medical school interviews, and see myself removing that thick envelope from the mailbox that had been sent by medical school X inviting me to join them for the 1986 (OMG!) entering class. I still use exercise as a stress reliever, and I still combine it with thinking about what I want in life. I really don't like to exercise. Sure, there's the feel-good part of it, once you've acquired some endurance, and yes, as a physician, I know it's supposed to be good for you, but, truth be known, I'd rather be doing something else. So, I try to combine exercise with an activity, like hiking in the mountains. I don't hike in the mountains for exercise per se. I like walking in the mountains and exploring places, and the exercise is a side, albeit important, benefit. I also like scuba diving. When I was a pre-med, I loved skiing and snowboarding as well. Often, exercise is the last thing we want to do. There will be days when you simply say no, but it's those days on which you must exercise, because those are typically the best workouts, and those are the days that will help you develop self-discipline that will serve you for a lifetime. **You** must exercise. It's the most difficult habit to make, and the easiest to break. For most of us, until we attain endurance, it's grueling at first. Overcoming the inertia and devoting that half hour a day (yes, just 30 minutes a day is all it takes) is sometimes difficult. But, those endogenous endorphins feel good, make you self-righteous, motivate you to stay focused, help deter you from eating junk food, improve your sleep, and keep you out of trouble with booze and other intoxicants. Yes, exercise is a miracle activity. Don't even try to give me excuses, because I've used, and/or heard, them all.

In order to maximize the benefits of your workout, get a heart monitor. It's the only way **You** can objectively measure whether you're giving yourself enough, but not too much, cardiovascular fitness. As you age, I suggest using additional time for stretching and muscle strengthening. The habits **You** make now will continue to serve you well as the stress of becoming a physician worsens in medical school and post-med-school training.

Discover an activity that **You** enjoy, and combine it with exercise. Do **You** like reading novels? Then get on an exercise bike and read one. Use the workout time for visualization. Make the habit… it will serve **You** well.

21 YOU ARE WHAT YOU EAT?!*
OJMJ!

"If Oprah, with her $2.7 billion, cannot lose weight and eat properly, then how can I?" **You** ask. That's a great excuse and rationalization. How can one argue it? Eating right, eating healthy, and being disciplined, especially with food, is a difficult, and for some, near impossible task. I know. I've had my own issues with food…still do, always will. I love to cook and eat. For me, both are relaxing, enjoyable and psychologically therapeutic.

If you don't already know how, learn to cook. Start cooking with wine. Have you ever fried something like meat in a skillet and then put wine into the hot skillet? Try it sometime, and watch the charred remains that are stuck to the skillet magically disappear. It's called deglazing. What do you think a little wine can do for your arteries if it deglazes a frying pan? Perhaps that's one of the reasons the French, with their amazingly delicious foods, soaked in butter and wine, have a lower incidence of heart disease than our fast-food-consuming nation. Is there something they put in fast food that causes addiction? Decades ago, this question was posed to the tobacco/cigarette industry, and it sounded just as silly then as this question does now.

Take a look online at the 'Happy Meal Experiment.' There are a number of links demonstrating the unchanged nature of the burger and fries after months spent sitting on the kitchen counter. Some reports say no flies landed on them, either! Stay away from fast food establishments. This advice comes from someone who, while a starving student at LA Valley College, lived on one-dollar Whopper Juniors for months during an especially lean financial period. I didn't know how to cook then either, but there are ways other than McDonald's to eat cheaply…much more healthy ways. And now, even McDonald's is offering oatmeal for breakfast and salads for lunch and dinner. As I stated before, I'm an advocate of everything in moderation, but for most of us, fast food, especially the classics (Big Macs, Whoppers, fries) becomes a very addictive habit that's as hard to break as the habit of exercise is to make.

Eating healthy takes more time and money, but the payoff is substantial. In case I haven't said this before: The habits **You** make now will serve you well (or not) as the stress of becoming a physician worsens in medical school and post-med-school training.

22 | FUN AND GAMES — R & R

"For six days, work is to be done, but the seventh day is a Sabbath of rest, holy to the LORD. Whoever does any work on the Sabbath day must be put to death." Exodus, 31:15

Wow, that's intense, huh? Gee, what if I'm a doctor and somebody gets injured or becomes ill on the Sabbath? Let 'em die, right?

It's interesting to see people change their minds about various aspects of organized religion and its teachings, especially once their child, or a loved one is involved. I doubt anybody is going to tell the doctor who is literally saving their child's life on Sunday that the doctor should not work. Hmmm, how does that really work then? Feel free to send us your thoughts on this to www.doctorberry.com.

Perhaps we should consider another angle:

"All work and no play leads to Regrat behavior." doctorberry, January 27, 2011

"You can discover more about a person in an hour of play than in a year of conversation." Plato

So, after all I've said about limiting your sexual encounters, eliminating your booze and other intoxicant ingestion, engaging yourself in exercise, limiting your ingestion of unhealthy foods, and concentrating on studying…I wanted to end with a very brief statement about adding a teeny, tiny, li'l bit a fun to your challenging life path. But, first, one qualifying paragraph:

If **You** are truly wanting to be a doctor because **You** are passionate about being a physician and it is what **You** believe **You** were born to do, then **You** are already having fun and games every day. As grueling as a pre-med and subsequent medical school, post-grad, blah, blah, blah, blee, blee, blee, life path is — and has been for me — I've had a terrific ride, and wouldn't change a thing. I enjoyed studying math, chemistry, physics, and medicine. I hated the stress of exams, and who doesn't, but overall, I still would have done it, even if I'd won the lottery. Now, some ideas for fun and games.

Plan one day a week, except the week before finals or boards, to get away from all the stress, joy and mental thrill of academics. Plan that day, and stick to it. Do something that's fun, and clear your mind. Go to an amusement park and feel the thrill of hurling your body around safely at high speed on a rollercoaster. I wasn't that smart.

I jumped off cliffs with snow skis strapped to my feet. I climbed mountains. Not hike mountains. I mean really climbed — thousands of feet, almost straight up, with ropes and everything. And I did other adrenaline junkie stuff that would have been just as easily and more safely replaced by riding on rollercoasters. Luckily, I survived.

The main point here is to plan for one day a week of rest. If R & R is not planned, it will take on its own life when least convenient, and if put off for too long, will manifest in self-destructive behavior.

essential advice for pre-meds

23 FRIENDS AND 'FRENEMIES'

Carol was smart, attractive, and popular in high school, but drowning at UCLA. We were in a number of classes together. Although we didn't hang out together, we'd talked many times about grades and MCAT scores. One afternoon, while I was sitting outside enjoying the perpetual LA sunshine near UCLA's biomolecular building and filling out medical school applications, Carol walked up and peered over my shoulder. "Oh my God!" (we didn't have 'OMG' back then) she said in her Valley Girl twang. "I don't know why YOU are applying to Harvard!" she continued.

"Well, if I don't apply to Harvard, I know I won't get in," I replied, annoyed. Carol was/is a great example of a 'frenemy,' a gunner, and, forgive me, a bitch.

The purple foxglove plant produces one of the most potent medicines still in use today, digitalis, a drug that is used for cardiac arrhythmias. Very low quantities are required to produce the desired effect in regulating heart rhythm, i.e., it has what's called a narrow therapeutic window. A little bit saves a person's life, a little more kills them.

It requires great courage to stand up against enemies, but it requires much more effort to stand up against your friends. Hence the term 'frenemies.' Like digitalis, 'frenemies' have a narrow therapeutic window. A 'frenemy' can be potent, highly effective medicine — in small doses.

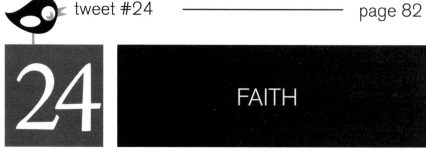

24

FAITH

"Sometimes you just have to take the leap and build your wings on the way down." Kobi Yamada

That's what I did. I decided to become a physician at a time when I had no job, no money, no high-school diploma, no family to rely upon, and no 'friends' who were in any way supportive. And yet I made the decision, somehow knowing it was the path I was supposed to travel, and built my wings as I went along. It was very difficult, especially those first few years. **You** have picked up this book because…why? **You** are thinking about becoming a doctor? **You** have already applied to medical school? **You** like the idea of applying these principles to your everyday life? It doesn't matter whether you're just starting high school, your grandchildren are just starting high school, or if you're 100+ years young. Faith is the key to living the rest of your life more fulfilled.

"For verily I say unto you, That whosoever shall say unto this mountain, Be thou removed, and be thou cast into the sea; and shall not doubt in his heart, but shall believe that those things which he saith shall come to pass; he shall have whatsoever he saith.

Therefore I say unto you, What things soever ye desire, when ye pray, believe that ye receive them, and ye shall have them." The Bible, King James Version, Mark 11:23 — 24

Believe in yourself and believe in following **Your** life path…

You will be the only one walking it.

25

IS THIS WHAT YOU REALLY, REALLY, REALLY WANT? — The Lottery Test

In the movie *Harry Potter and the Sorcerer's Stone*, Headmaster Dumbledore comes upon Harry sitting in front of the Mirror of Erised. He tells Harry that, "The happiest man on earth would look into the mirror and see only himself, exactly as he is."

Harry responds by saying, "It shows us what we want, whatever we want."

"Yes, and no," Dumbledore replies patiently, then continues. "Nothing more or less than the deepest and most desperate desires of our hearts."

If **You** stood in front of the Mirror of Erised, would you see yourself standing there in scrubs and a white coat with a stethoscope around your neck? If, without hesitation, you answer yes, then put this book down immediately, vamoose, and lucubrate. If you answer no, or have other things in mind, or seem to have reservations, I warn you – the pursuit of medical school, medical school itself, the post-medical-school training and the practice of medicine may not be worth the effort, the money, and the ultimate expense of years of your life. Let's try something else.

If you won the lottery today, say $90 million (after tax, cash), would you still want to be a doctor? When I had my epiphany that New Year's Eve in 1979 that I was going to transform from high-school dropout to physician, it was as if I was standing in front of the Mirror of Erised, and there I was. I was wearing scrubs and a white coat, and had a stethoscope around my neck. It was some years later, while counseling a patient, that I developed the 'Lottery Test,' and I still use it today to help guide me towards decisions that reflect my deepest, most desperate desires. Becoming a doctor would have withstood that test.

Does it for **You**?

INDEX

25tweets   essential advice for pre-meds

25tweets   essential advice for pre-meds

Author's Note

This book was written to provide you with real world useful information. I wrote the kind of book that I wish I had available (I bought every book) during those trying, difficult and sometimes depressing days/weeks/ months of undergrad. The reproduction of my transcripts, the telling of my personal experiences and the psychological difficulties endured during the waxing/waning "dark" times are all shared here to provide you with a reference book that you can turn to, over and over, to compare your grades, MCAT scores, experiences with professors and classmates with someone (ME) that has - 'been there, done that.' The chapters dealing with inspirational and other behavioral issues are just as important as the more practical chapters about grades, scores and interviews - use them and heed the warnings.

I used the bold, capitalized and underlined "**You**" as a way to emphasize that this book and its information is for you. That you are not alone in whatever feelings you may have, whatever grades you may have and, whatever life situation you may currently find yourself.

There are more intensive treatments of school selection, interviews, grades, habits and inspiration on my web site:

doctorberry.com

Finally, there are others who may benefit from this book and only need to discover it. Don't keep it to yourself. We are too competitive as pre-meds and physicians and that has polarized us, causing doctor's to lose control of the practice of medicine to politicians and "business" types. So, help out a fellow classmate/friend (and me) by taking a picture of the book cover and Facebook it, email it, text it, to others.

Good Luck and remember:

If I Did It, So Can **You**!

doctorberry

(PaulS. Berry, MD, JD, MBA)

 25tweets   essential advice for pre-meds